Essential Angular

An overview of the key aspects written by two of the Angular core contributors

Victor Savkin
Jeff Cross

BIRMINGHAM - MUMBAI

Essential Angular

First published: May 2017

Production reference: 1300517

Published by Packt Publishing Ltd.
Livery Place
35 Livery Street
Birmingham
B3 2PB, UK.
ISBN 978-1-78829-376-1

www.packtpub.com

Credits

Authors
Victor Savkin
Jeff Cross

Acquisition Editor
Ben Renow-Clarke

Indexer
Mariammal Chettiyar

Technical Editor
Bhagyashree Rai

Production Coordinator
Shraddha Falebhai

About the Authors

Victor Savkin and Jeff Cross are core contributors to the Angular projects.

Victor Savkin has been on the Angular team since the inception of Angular 2. Victor developed dependency injection, change detection, forms, and the router.

Jeff Cross was one of the earliest core team members on Angular 1. He developed the Angular 2 HTTP and AngularFire2 modules, contributed to RxJS 5, and was most recently the Tech Lead of the Angular Mobile team at Google.

Nrwl.io – Angular consulting for enterprise customers, from core team members

Victor and Jeff are founder of Nrwl, a company providing Angular consulting for enterprise customers, from core team members. Visit `nrwl.io` for more information.

www.PacktPub.com

For support files and downloads related to your book, please visit www.PacktPub.com.

Did you know that Packt offers eBook versions of every book published, with PDF and ePub files available? You can upgrade to the eBook version at www.PacktPub.comand as a print book customer, you are entitled to a discount on the eBook copy. Get in touch with us at service@packtpub.com for more details.

At www.PacktPub.com, you can also read a collection of free technical articles, sign up for a range of free newsletters and receive exclusive discounts and offers on Packt books and eBooks.

https://www.packtpub.com/mapt

Get the most in-demand software skills with Mapt. Mapt gives you full access to all Packt books and video courses, as well as industry-leading tools to help you plan your personal development and advance your career.

Why subscribe?

- Fully searchable across every book published by Packt
- Copy and paste, print, and bookmark content
- On demand and accessible via a web browser

Customer Feedback

Thanks for purchasing this Packt book. At Packt, quality is at the heart of our editorial process. To help us improve, please leave us an honest review on this book's Amazon page at `https://www.amazon.com/dp/1788293762`.

If you'd like to join our team of regular reviewers, you can e-mail us at `customerreviews@packtpub.com`. We award our regular reviewers with free eBooks and videos in exchange for their valuable feedback. Help us be relentless in improving our products!

Table of Contents

Preface 1

Example 5

Chapter 1: Compilation 7

    JIT and AOT 8

    Why would I want to do it? 9

    How is it possible? 9

    Trade-offs 10

    Let's recap 11

Chapter 2: NgModules 13

    Declarations, imports, and exports 13

        Summary 14

    Bootstrap and entry components 14

        Summary 17

    Providers 17

    Injecting NgModules and module initialization 17

    Bootstrap 18

    Lazy loading 19

    Let's recap 20

Chapter 3: Components and Directives 21

    Input and output properties 22

    Template 23

    Life cycle 24

    Providers 25

    Host element 25

    Queries 27

    Let's recap 28

    What about directives? 28

Chapter 4: Templates 29

    Why templates? 29

        Swapping implementations 30

        Analyzing templates 30

        Transforming templates 30

Separating dynamic and static parts	31
Building on existing technologies and communities	31
Angular templates	32
Property and event bindings	32
Two-way bindings	33
Interpolation	33
Passing constants	34
References	34
Templates and *	34
Let's recap	35

Chapter 5: Dependency Injection — 37

Registering providers	39
Injector tree	40
Resolution	41
Lazy loading	42
Getting injector	43
Visualizing injector tree	44
Advanced topics	45
Controlling visibility	45
Optional dependencies	45
More on registering providers	46
Aliasing	47
Overrides	47
Let's recap	48

Chapter 6: Change Detection — 49

Two phases	49
Why?	52
Predictability	52
Performance	53
How does Angular enforce It?	53
Content and view children	54
ChangeDetectionStrategy.OnPush	55
Let's recap	56

Chapter 7: Forms — 57

Two modules	57
High-level overview	58
App model	58
Form model	58

Form directives   59
DOM   59
Form model   59
FormControl   60
FormGroup   60
FormArray   61
Updating form model   61
Disabling form model   63
Async validations   63
Composing validators   64
Listening to changes   65
Power of RxJS   66
Why form model?   66
Form directives   67
ReactiveFormsModule   67
FormsModule   69
Accessing form model when using FormsModule   72
The DOM   73
Wrapping up   74
Chapter 8: Testing   77
Isolated tests   77
Shallow testing   79
Integration testing   81
Protractor tests   83
Let's recap   84
Chapter 9: Reactive Programming in Angular   85
Reactive programming in the core framework   85
Events and state   86
Definition   86
Time   87
Reified and transparent   88
Observables   89
RxJS and reactive programming   89
What about event callbacks?   89
Reactive programming in the Angular ecosystem   90
@angular/forms   90
@angular/router   92
Summary   93
Index   95

Preface

What is this book about?

This book aims to be a short, but at the same time, fairly complete overview of the key aspects of Angular: it covers the framework's mental model, its API, and the design principles behind it.

To make one thing clear: this book is not a how-to-get-started guide. There is a lot of information about it available online. The goal of this book is different. Read this book after you toyed around with the framework, but before you embark on writing your first serious Angular application. The book will give you a strong foundation. It will help you put all the concepts into right places. So you will have a good understanding of why the framework is the way it is.

Let's get started!

Who this book is for

To get the most from this book, you should already have a good understanding of Angular and general web development. The book dives quickly into the core Angular systems without stepping through the basics.

Conventions

In this book, you will find a number of text styles that distinguish between different kinds of information. Here are some examples of these styles and an explanation of their meaning. Code words in text, database table names, folder names, filenames, file extensions, pathnames, dummy URLs, user input, and Twitter handles are shown as follows: "This will compile AppModule into a module factory and then use the factory to instantiate the module." A block of code is set as follows:

```
class TalkCmp {
  @Input() talk: Talk;
  @Output() rate: EventEmitter;
//...
}
```

When we wish to draw your attention to a particular part of a code block, the relevant lines or items are set in bold:

```
class TalkCmp {
@Input() talk: Talk;
  @Output() rate: EventEmitter;
//...
}
```

New terms and **important words** are shown in bold. Words that you see on the screen, for example, in menus or dialog boxes, appear in the text like this: "Say the conference application we use in this book has a **Load More** button, clicking on which loads more items and adds them to the list."

Warnings or important notes appear in a box like this.

Tips and tricks appear like this.

Reader feedback

Feedback from our readers is always welcome. Let us know what you think about this book-what you liked or disliked. Reader feedback is important for us as it helps us develop titles that you will really get the most out of. To send us general feedback, simply e-mail feedback@packtpub.com, and mention the book's title in the subject of your message. If there is a topic that you have expertise in and you are interested in either writing or contributing to a book, see our author guide at www.packtpub.com/authors.

Customer support

Now that you are the proud owner of a Packt book, we have a number of things to help you to get the most from your purchase.

Downloading the example code

You can download the example code files for this book from your account at `http://www.p acktpub.com`. If you purchased this book elsewhere, you can visit `http://www.packtpub.c om/support` and register to have the files e-mailed directly to you. You can download the code files by following these steps:

1. Log in or register to our website using your e-mail address and password.
2. Hover the mouse pointer on the **SUPPORT** tab at the top.
3. Click on **Code Downloads & Errata**.
4. Enter the name of the book in the **Search** box.
5. Select the book for which you're looking to download the code files.
6. Choose from the drop-down menu where you purchased this book from.
7. Click on **Code Download**.

Once the file is downloaded, please make sure that you unzip or extract the folder using the latest version of:

- WinRAR / 7-Zip for Windows
- Zipeg / iZip / UnRarX for Mac
- 7-Zip / PeaZip for Linux

The code bundle for the book is also hosted on GitHub at `https://github.com/PacktPubl ishing/Essential-Angular`. We also have other code bundles from our rich catalog of books and videos available at `https://github.com/PacktPublishing/`. Check them out!

Downloading the color images of this book

We also provide you with a PDF file that has color images of the screenshots/diagrams used in this book. The color images will help you better understand the changes in the output. You can download this file from `https://www.packtpub.com/sites/default/files/down loads/EssentialAngular_ColorImages.pdf`.

Errata

Although we have taken every care to ensure the accuracy of our content, mistakes do happen. If you find a mistake in one of our books-maybe a mistake in the text or the code-we would be grateful if you could report this to us. By doing so, you can save other readers from frustration and help us improve subsequent versions of this book. If you find any errata, please report them by visiting http://www.packtpub.com/submit-errata, selecting your book, clicking on the **Errata Submission Form** link, and entering the details of your errata. Once your errata are verified, your submission will be accepted and the errata will be uploaded to our website or added to any list of existing errata under the Errata section of that title. To view the previously submitted errata, go to https://www.packtpub.com/books/content/support and enter the name of the book in the search field. The required information will appear under the **Errata** section.

Piracy

Piracy of copyrighted material on the Internet is an ongoing problem across all media. At Packt, we take the protection of our copyright and licenses very seriously. If you come across any illegal copies of our works in any form on the Internet, please provide us with the location address or website name immediately so that we can pursue a remedy. Please contact us at copyright@packtpub.com with a link to the suspected pirated material. We appreciate your help in protecting our authors and our ability to bring you valuable content.

Questions

If you have a problem with any aspect of this book, you can contact us at questions@packtpub.com, and we will do our best to address the problem.

Example

For most of the examples in this book we will use the same application. This application is a list of tech talks that you can filter, watch, and rate.

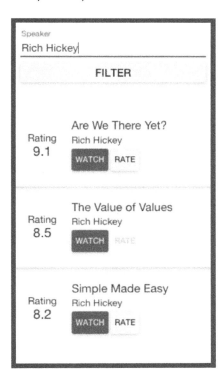

You can find the source code of the application here `https://github.com/vsavkin/essential-angular-book-app`.

1
Compilation

At the core of Angular is a sophisticated compiler, which takes a `NgModule` type and produces a `NgModuleFactory`.

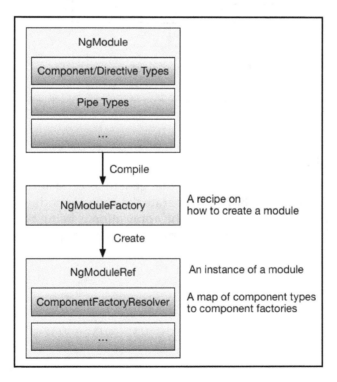

A NgModule has components declared in it. While creating the module factory, the compiler will take the template of every component in the module, and using the information about declared components and pipes, will produce a component factory. The component factory is a JavaScript class the framework can use to stamp out components.

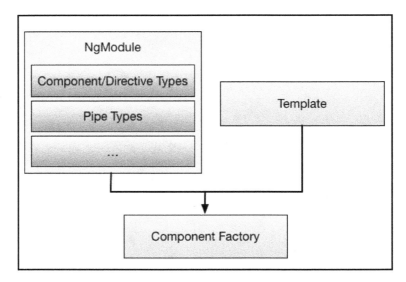

JIT and AOT

Angular 1 is a sophisticated HTML compiler that generates code at runtime. New versions of Angular have this option too: they can generate the code at runtime, or **Just-in-time** (**JIT**). In this case, the compilation happens while the application is being bootstrapped. But they also have another option: they can run the compiler as part of application's build, or **Ahead-of-time** (**AOT**).

Why would I want to do it?

Compiling your application ahead of time is beneficial for the following reasons:

- We no longer have to ship the compiler to the client. And so it happens, the compiler is the largest part of the framework. So it has a positive effect on the download size.
- Since the compiled app does not have any HTML and instead has the generated TypeScript code, the TypeScript compiler can analyze it to produce type errors. In other words, your templates are type safe.
- Bundlers (for example, WebPack and Rollup) can tree shake away everything that is not used in the application. This means that you no longer have to create 50-line node modules to reduce the download size of your application. The bundler will figure out which components are used, and the rest will be removed from the bundle.
- Finally, since the most expensive step in the bootstrap of your application is the compilation, compiling ahead of time can significantly improve the bootstrap time.

To sum up, using the AOT compilation makes your application bundles smaller, faster, and safer.

How is it possible?

Why did not we do it before, in Angular 1? To make AOT work the application has to have a clear separation of the static and dynamic data in the application. And the compiler has to built in such a way that it only depends on the static data. When designing and building Angular we put a lot of effort to do exactly that. And such primitives as classes and decorators, which the new versions of JavaScript and TypeScript support, made it way easier.

To see how this separation works in practice, let's look at the following example. Here, the information in the decorator is known statically. Angular knows the selector and the template of the `talk` component. It also knows that the component has an input called `talk` and an output called `rate`. But the framework does not know what the constructor or the `onRate` function do.

```
@Component({
  selector: 'talk-cmp',
  template: `
    {{talk.title}} {{talk.speaker}}
    Rating: {{ talk.rating | formatRating }}
    <watch-button [talk]="talk"></watch-button>
    <rate-button [talk]="talk" (click)="onRate()"></rate-button>
  `
})
class TalkCmp {
  @Input() talk: Talk;
  @Output() rate: EventEmitter;

  constructor() {
    // some initialization logic
  }

  onRate() {
    // reacting to a rate event
  }
}
```

Since Angular knows all the necessary information ahead of time, it can compile this component without actually executing any application code, as a build step.

Trade-offs

Since AOT is so advantageous, we recommend to use it in production. But, as with everything, there are trade-offs. For Angular to be able to compile your application ahead of time, the metadata has to be statically analyzable. For instance, the following code will not work in the AOT mode:

```
@Component({
  selector: 'talk-cmp',
  template: () => window.hide ? 'hidden' : `
    {{talk.title}} {{talk.speaker}}
    Rating: {{ talk.rating | formatRating }}
    <watch-button [talk]="talk"></watch-button>
    <rate-button [talk]="talk" (click)="onRate()"></rate-button>
  `
})
class TalkCmp {
  //...
}
```

The `window.hide` property will not be defined. So the compilation will fail to point out the error. A lot of work has been done to make the compiler smarter, so it can understand most of the day-to-day patterns you would use when building your application. But certain things will never work, like the preceding example.

Let's recap

- The central part of Angular is its compiler.
- The compilation can be done just in time (at runtime) and ahead of time (as a build step).
- The AOT compilation creates smaller bundles, tree shakes dead code, makes your templates type-safe, and improves the bootstrap time of your application.
- The AOT compilation requires certain metadata to be known statically, so the compilation can happen without actually executing the code.

2
NgModules

Declarations, imports, and exports

NgModules are the unit of compilation and distribution of Angular components and pipes. In many ways, they are similar to ES6 modules, in that they have declarations, imports, and exports.

Let's look at this example:

```
@NgModule({
  declarations: [FormattedRatingPipe, WatchButtonCmp, \
    RateButtonCmp, TalkCmp, TalksCmp],
  exports: [TalksCmp]
})
class TalksModule {}

@NgModule({
  declarations: [AppCmp],
  imports: [BrowserModule, TalksModule],
  bootstrap: [AppCmp]
})
class AppModule {}
```

Here we define two modules: TalksModule and AppModule. TalksModule has all the components and pipes that do actual work in the application, whereas AppModule has only AppCmp, which is a thin application shell.

`TalksModule` declares four components and one pipe. The four components can use each other in their templates, similar to how classes defined in an ES module can refer to each other in their methods. Also, all the components can use `FormattedRatingPipe`. So an `NgModule` is the compilation context of its components, that is, it tells Angular how these components should be compiled. As with ES, a component can only be declared in one module.

In this example `TalksModule` exports only `TalksCmp`—the rest is private. This means that only `TalksCmp` is added to the compilation context of `AppModule`. Again this is similar to how the `export` keyword works in JavaScript.

Summary

- NgModules are akin to ES modules: they have declarations, imports, and exports.
- NgModules define the compilation context of their components.

Bootstrap and entry components

The `bootstrap` property defines the components that are instantiated when a module is bootstrapped. First, Angular creates a component factory for each of the bootstrap components. And then, at runtime, it'll use the factories to instantiate the components.

To generate less code, and, as a result, to produce smaller bundles, Angular won't generate component factories for any components of `TalksModule`. The framework can see their usage statically, it can inline their instantiation, so no factories are required. This is true for any component used statically (or declaratively) in the template.

For instance, let's look at `TalkCmp`:

```
@Component({
  selector: 'talk-cmp',
  template: `
    {{talk.title}} {{talk.speaker}}
    {{talk.rating | formatRating}}
    <watch-button [talk]="talk"></watch-button>
    <rate-button [talk]="talk"></rate-button>
  `
})
class TalkCmp {
  @Input() talk: Talk;
  @Output() rate: EventEmitter;
  //...
}
```

Angular knows, at compile time, that `TalkCmp` uses `WatchButtonCmp` and `RateButtonCmp`, so it can instantiate them directly, without any indirection or extra abstractions.

Now let's look at a different component that uses the router:

```
@Component({
  selector: 'router-cmp',
  template: `
    <router-outlet></router-outlet>
  `
})
class RouterCmp {}

@NgModule({
  declarations: [RouterCmp],
  imports: [BrowserModule, RouterModule, TalksModule],
  bootstrap: [RouterCmp],
  providers: [
    {provide: ROUTES, useValue: [
      { path: 'talks', component: TalksCmp },
      { path: 'settings', component: SettingsCmp }
    ]}
  ]
})
class RouterModule {}
```

Angular cannot statically figure out what components can be loaded into the outlet, and, as a result, cannot instantiate them directly. Here we need the extra abstraction, we need the component factories for both `TalksCmp` and `SettingsCmp`. We can tell Angular to generate those by listing them as entry components.

```
@NgModule({
  declarations: [RouterCmp],
  imports: [BrowserModule, RouterModule, TalksModule],
  bootstrap: [RouterCmp],
  entryComponents: [TalksCmp, SettingsCmp],
  providers: [
    {provide: ROUTES, useValue: [
      { path: 'talks', component: TalksCmp },
      { path: 'settings', component: SettingsCmp }
    ]}
  ]
})
class RouterModule {}
```

Even though we do not use `TalksCmp` or `SettingsCmp` in any template, the router configuration is still static. And it is cumbersome to declare every component used by the router in the entry components. Because this is so common, Angular supports a special provider token to automatically pre-populate `entryComponents`.

```
@NgModule({
  declarations: [RouterCmp],
  imports: [BrowserModule, RouterModule, TalksModule],
  bootstrap: [RouterCmp],
  providers: [
    {provide: ROUTES, useValue: [
        { path: 'talks', component: TalksCmp },
        { path: 'settings', component: SettingsCmp }
    ]},
    {provide: ANALYZE_FOR_ENTRY_COMPONENTS, multi: true, \
    useExisting: ROUTES}
  ]
})
class RouterModule {}
```

And when using `RouterModule.forRoot` or `RouterModule.forChild`, the router module takes care of it.

```
@NgModule({
  declarations: [RouterCmp],
  imports: [BrowserModule, TalksModule, RouterModule.forRoot([
    { path: 'talks', components: TalksCmp },
    { path: 'settings', components: SettingsCmp }
  ])],
  bootstrap: [RouterCmp]
})
class RouterModule {}
```

Summary

- To be more efficient, Angular separates components used statically (declaratively) from the components used dynamically (imperatively)
- Angular directly instantiates components used statically; no extra abstraction is required
- Angular generates a component factory for every component listed in `entryComponents` so that they can be instantiated imperatively

Providers

I'll cover providers and dependency injection in Chapter 5, *Dependency Injection*. Here I'd like to just note that NgModules can contain providers. And the providers of the imported modules are merged with the target module's providers, left to right, that is, if multiple imported modules define the same provider, the last module wins.

```
@NgModule({
  providers: [
    Repository
  ]
})
class TalksModule {}

@NgModule({
  imports: [TalksModule]
})
class AppModule {}
```

Injecting NgModules and module initialization

Angular instantiates NgModules and registers them with dependency injection. This means that you can inject modules into other modules or components, like this:

```
@NgModule({
  imports: [TalksModule]
})
class AppModule {
  constructor(t: TalksModule) {}
}
```

This can be useful for coordinating the initialization of multiple modules, as shown here:

```
@NgModule({
  imports: [ModuleA, ModuleB]
})
class AppModule {
  constructor(a: ModuleA, b: ModuleB) {
    a.initialize().then(() => b.initialize());
  }
}
```

Bootstrap

To bootstrap an Angular application in the JIT mode, you pass a module to `bootstrapModule`:

```
import {platformBrowserDynamic} from '@angular/platform-browser-dynamic';
import {AppModule} from './app';

platformBrowserDynamic().bootstrapModule(AppModule);
```

This will compile `AppModule` into a module factory and then use the factory to instantiate the module. If you use AOT, you may need to provide the factory yourself:

```
import {platformBrowser} from '@angular/platform-browser';
import {AppModuleNgFactory} from './app.ngfactory';

platformBrowser().bootstrapModuleFactory(AppModuleNgFactory);
```

I said "may need to" because the CLI and the WebPack plugin take care of it for you. They will replace the `bootstrapModule` call with `bootstrapModuleFactory` when needed.

Lazy loading

As I mentioned earlier NgModules are not just the units of compilation, they are also the units of distribution. That is why we bootstrap a NgModule, and not a component—we don't distribute components, we distribute modules. And that's why we lazy load NgModules as well.

```
import {NgModuleFactoryLoader, Injector} from '@angular/core';

class MyService {
  constructor(loader: NgModuleFactoryLoader, injector: Injector) {
    loader.load("mymodule").then((f: NgModuleFactory) => {
      const moduleRef = f.create(injector);
      moduleRef.injector; // module injector
      moduleRef.componentFactoryResolver; // all the \
components factories of the lazy-loaded module
    });
  }
}
```

The loader compiles the modules if the application is running in the JIT mode, and does not in the AOT mode. The default loader `@angular/core` ships with uses SystemJS, but, as most things in Angular, you can provide your own.

Let's recap

- NgModules are the units of compilation. They tell Angular how components should be compiled.
- Similar to ES module they have declarations, imports, and exports.
- Every component belongs to a NgModule.
- Bootstrap and entry components are configured in NgModules.
- NgModules configure dependency injection.
- NgModules are used to bootstrap applications.
- NgModules are used to lazy load code.

3
Components and Directives

To build an Angular application you define a set of components, for every UI element, screen, and route. An application will always have root components (usually just one) that contain all other components. To make things simpler, in this book let's assume the application has a single root component, and thus our Angular application will have a component tree, that may look like this:

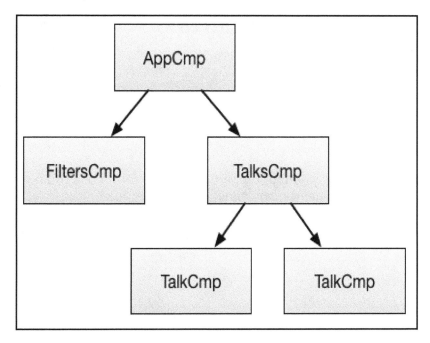

AppCmp is the root component. The FiltersCmp component has the speaker input and the filter button. TalksCmp is the list you see at the bottom. And TalkCmp is an item in that list. To understand what constitutes a component in Angular, let's look closer at TalkCmp:

```
@Component({
  selector: 'talk-cmp',
  template: `
    {{talk.title}} {{talk.speaker}}
    {{talk.rating | formatRating }}
    <watch-button [talk]="talk"></watch-button>
    <rate-button [talk]="talk"></rate-button>
  `
})
class TalkCmp {
  @Input() talk: Talk;
  @Output() rate: EventEmitter;
  //...
}
```

Input and output properties

A component has input and output properties, which can be defined in the component decorator or using property decorators.

```
class TalkCmp {
  @Input() talk: Talk;
  @Output() rate: EventEmitter;
  //...
}
```

Data flows into a component via input properties. Data flows out of a component via output properties, hence the names: input and output.

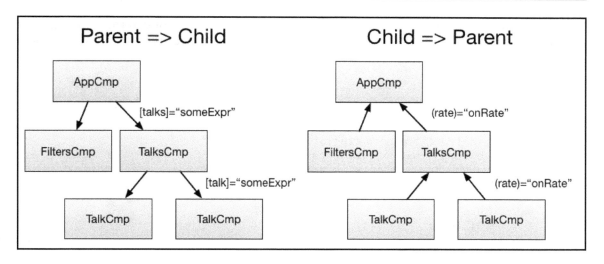

Input and output properties are the public API of a component. You use them when you instantiate a component in your application.

```
<talk-cmp [talk]="someExp" (rate)="onRate($event.rating)"></talk-cmp>;
```

You can set input properties using property bindings, through square brackets. You can subscribe to output properties using event bindings, through parenthesis.

Template

A component has a template, which describes how the component is rendered on the page.

```
@Component({
  selector: 'talk-cmp',
  template: `
    {{talk.title}} {{talk.speaker}}
    {{talk.rating | formatRating}}
    <watch-button [talk]="talk"></watch-button>
    <rate-button [talk]="talk"></rate-button>
  `
})
class TalkCmp {}
```

You can define the template inline, as shown in the preceding code, or externally using `templateUrl`. In addition to the template, a component can define styles using the `styles` and `styleUrls` properties.

```
@Component({
  selector: 'talk-cmp',
  template: `
    {{talk.title}} {{talk.speaker}}
    {{talk.rating | formatRating}}
    <watch-button [talk]="talk"></watch-button>
    <rate-button [talk]="talk"></rate-button>
  `,
  styles: [`
    watch-button {
      margin: 10px;
    }
  `]
})
class TalkCmp {}
```

By default the styles are encapsulated, so the margin defined in the preceding code won't affect any other component using `watch-button`.

Life cycle

Components have a well-defined life cycle, which you can tap into. `TalkCmp` does not subscribe to any life cycle events, but some other components can. For instance, this component will be notified when its input properties change.

```
@Component({
  selector: 'cares-about-changes'
})
class CaresAboutChanges implements OnChanges {
  @Input() field1;
  @Input() field2;

  ngOnChanges(changes) { //.. }
}
```

Providers

A component can configure dependency injection by defining the list of providers the component and its children may inject.

```
@Component({
    selector: 'conf-app',
    providers: [Logger]
})
class AppCmp { //... }

@Component({
    ...
})
class TalksCmp {
    constructor(logger:Logger) { //... }
}
```

In this example, we have the logger service declared in the app component, which makes them available in the whole application. The talks component injects the logger service. I will cover dependency injection in detail in Chapter 5, *Dependency Injection*. For now, just remember that components can configure dependency injection.

Host element

To turn an Angular component into something rendered in the DOM you have to associate an Angular component with a DOM element. We call such elements host elements.

A component can interact with its host DOM element in the following ways:

- It can listen to its events
- It can update its properties
- It can invoke methods on it

The component, for instance, listens to the input event using `hostListeners`, trims the value, and then stores it in a field. Angular will sync up the stored value with the DOM.

```
@Directive({
  selector: '[trimmed-input]'
})
class TrimmedInput {
  @HostBinding() value: string;

  @HostListener("input", "$event.target.value")
  onChange(updatedValue: string) {
    this.value = updatedValue.trim();
  }
}
```

Note, I don't actually interact with the DOM directly. Angular aims to provide a higher-level API, so the native platform, the DOM, will just reflect the state of the Angular application. This is useful for a couple of reasons:

- It makes components easier to refactor.
- It allows unit testing most of the behavior of an application without touching the DOM. Such tests are easier to write and understand. In addition, they are significantly faster.
- It allows running Angular applications in a web worker, server, or other platforms where a native DOM isn't present.
- Sometimes you just need to interact with the DOM directly. Angular provides such APIs, but our hope is that you will rarely need to use them.

Queries

In addition, to access its host element, a component can interact with its children. There are two types of children a component can have: **content children** and **view children**. To understand the difference between them, let's look at the following example:

```
@Component({
  selector: 'tab',
  template: `...`
})
class TabCmp {}

@Component({
  selector: 'tabs',
  template: `
    Tabs:
    <div>
      <ng-content></ng-content>
    </div>
    <div>
      <button (click)="selectPrev()">Prev</button>
      <button (click)="selectNext()">Next</button>
    </div>
  `
})
class TabsCmp {}

@Component({
  template: `
    <tabs>
      <tab ></tab>
      <tab title="Two"></tab>
      <tab ></tab>
    </tabs>
  `
})
class CmpUsingTabs {
}
```

The content children of the `tabs` component are the three `tab` components. The user of the `tabs` component provided those. The previous and next buttons are the view children of the `tabs` component. The author of the `tabs` component provided those. Components can query their children using the `ContentChild`, `ContentChildren`, `ViewChild`, and `ViewChildren` decorators.

Angular will set this list during the construction of the `tabs` component and will keep it updated when content children get created, removed, or reordered. I will talk more about this in `Chapter 5`, *Dependency Injection*.

Let's recap

What I have listed constitutes a component.

- A component knows how to interact with its host element
- A component knows how to interact with its content and view children
- A component knows how to render itself
- A component configures dependency injection
- A component has a well-defined public API of input and output properties

All of these make components in Angular self-describing, so they contain all the information needed to instantiate them. And this is extremely important.

This means that any component can be bootstrapped. It does not have to be special in any way. Moreover, any component can be loaded into a router outlet. As a result, you can write a component that can be bootstrapped as an application, loaded as a route, or used in some other component directly. This results in less API to learn. And it also makes components more reusable.

What about directives?

If you are familiar with Angular 1, you must be wondering "What happened to directives?".

Actually, directives are still here in Angular. The component is just the most important type of a directive, but not the only one. A component is a directive with a template. But you can still write decorator-style directives, which do not have templates.

4
Templates

In modern web development, there are two main techniques for describing what components render: using JavaScript and using templates. In this chapter I will talk about why Angular uses templates, and how its templates work.

Why templates?

Before we jump into how, let's talk about why.

Using templates is aligned with the rule of least power, which is a useful design principle.

> *the less powerful the language, the more you can do with the data stored in that language. [...] I chose HTML not to be a programming language because I wanted different programs to do different things with it: present it differently, extract tables of contents, index it, and so on.*

> *–Tim Berners-Lee, on the Principle of Least Power*

 For the full article refer https://www.w3.org/DesignIssues/Principles.html#PLP

Because templates are pure HTML, and hence are constrained, tools and developers can make smart assumptions about what components are and how they behave, and Angular can do a lot of interesting things that would have not been possible if components used JavaScript instead. Let's look at some of those.

Swapping implementations

Performance is tricky: often it is hard to know ahead of time how well a particular technique will work. In addition, what is performant right now may not be as performant in the future: browsers evolve.

One of the best things templates give us is a clear boundary separating the view layer from the rest of the framework, so we swap the implementation of the view layer without breaking any applications. This allows us to experiment and adapt the framework to new capabilities of the platform.

Finally, the framework can have multiple implementations of the template compiler optimized for different use cases (for example, mobile vs desktop).

Analyzing templates

Being able to analyze templates is another consequence of the rule of least power.

Imagine we use a data-access library like Falcor (`http://netflix.github.io/falcor/`) or Apollo (`https://github.com/apollographql/apollo-angular`).

Normally, we would have to define all the queries needed by those libraries explicitly. And if we do not use templates, there is not much we can do about it. It is not possible, at least in a general way, to derive the queries from the JavaScript code rendering the components without actually running it.

The situation is different when the framework uses templates. They are much simpler, and more constrained than JavaScript, and, as a result, the data-access integration library could reliably derive the queries from the templates. And since the queries usually match the structure of the templates pretty closely (after all the templates are showing the data returned by the queries), we can remove a lot of duplication this way.

Transforming templates

What is even more powerful than template introspection is the ability to transform templates during compilation. And yes, it's possible to transform JavaScript with, let's say, a Babel plugin, but it is a lot harder too, at least if we want to do it correctly.

Templating languages are different. They just define the structure of the view and have a limited set of well-defined side effects. That is why automatically adding new things to the template is unlikely to break the guarantees the templating language provides.

Here is an analogy to give you an intuition of what I mean here. Using templates to render components is akin to using this array literal [1,20,2,4] to describe the collection of the four numbers. Using JavaScript to render components is similar to using the following instructions to describe the same collection:

```
array.push(1);
array.push(20);
array.push(21);
array.pop();
array.push(2);
array.push(4);
```

Yes, the resulting collection is the same. The difference is that we can analyze the literal statically. So it is a lot easier to write transformations of it. And though in simple cases it is possible to analyze JavaScript to figure out what the resulting array will look like, it is not trivial. And it is not possible for an arbitrary set of instructions.

Separating dynamic and static parts

Another thing that using a templating language gives us is a clear separation of the dynamic and static parts of the view. Angular can easily see what parts of the view are static and optimize those. For instance, Angular knows that only expressions can cause changes in the DOM, and the rest of the markup is static. So after the initial rendering is done, the static markup is essentially free.

Building on existing technologies and communities

Finally, a lot of people are already proficient with HTML and CSS, and they can leverage this knowledge to write HTML templates. On top of that, there is a rich set of tools around these technologies, and being able to use them when building applications is a huge plus.

Angular templates

Templates *can* be analyzable, transformable, and declarative in a way that JavaScript *fundamentally* cannot be. When designing Angular we put a lot of effort to make sure the template language has these properties. Let's look at what we ended up with.

Property and event bindings

Input and output properties are the public API of a directive. Data flows into a directive via its inputs and flows out via its outputs. We can update input properties using property bindings. And we can subscribe to output properties using event bindings.

Say we have a component that renders a button that allows rating a conference talk. We could use this component in our template as follows:

```
<rate-button [talk]="myTalk" (rate)="handleRate($event)"></rate-button>
```

This tells Angular that whenever `myTalk` changes, Angular needs to automatically update the `rate-button` component by calling the setter. This also tells Angular that if an event called `rate` is fired, it should invoke `handleRate`.

Now, let's look at the `RateButtonCmp` class:

```
@Component({
  selector: 'rate-button',
  templateUrl: './rate-button.component.html',
  styleUrls: ['./rate-button.component.css']
})
export class RateButtonCmp {
  @Input() talk: Talk;
  @Output() rate = new EventEmitter();

  promptRating(): void {
    const value = prompt("Enter rating");
    if (value) {
      this.rate.next(+value);
    }
  }
}
```

The component declares that it has an input property named `talk` and an output property `rate`. Only the input properties of a component can be updated using property bindings. This separates the input of the component from its internal state.

Angular uses the Rx style of programming to deal with events. `EventEmitter` is an implementation of both the observable and observer interfaces. So we can use it to fire events, and Angular can use it to listen to events.

As you can see, the core syntax of property and event bindings is very simple. On top of the core syntax, Angular provides some syntax sugar to make expressing common programming patterns easier. It is important to understand that this is just sugar, and it does not change the semantics.

Two-way bindings

Two-way data bindings are convenient in certain scenarios, most notably for handling input. As I have mentioned, property bindings are used to pass data from the parent to the child, and event bindings are used to pass data from the child to the parent. So we can use the two together to implement two-way bindings.

```
<input [ngModel]="todo.text" (ngModelChange)="todo.text=$event">
```

Although this works, this is too verbose. And since this is such a common pattern, Angular provides syntax sugar to remove the boilerplate.

```
<input [(ngModel)]="todo.text"></input>
```

Interpolation

```
<div>Rating {{rating}}</div>
```

is just sugar for:

```
<div [textContent]="interpolate(['Rating'], [rating])"></div>
```

Passing constants

```
<input md-input formControlName="title">
```

is just sugar for:

```
<input md-input [formControlName]=" 'title' ">
```

References

It is not uncommon to have two components that have to talk to each other. To enable that Angular supports defining references in the template.

```
<confirmation-dialog #dialog></confirmation-dialog>
<button (click)="dialog.open()">Open</button>
```

The references get hoisted, so their order does not matter.

Templates and *

Angular treats template elements in a special way. They are used to create views, chunks of DOM you can dynamically manipulate. The * syntax is a shortcut that lets you avoid writing the whole element. Let me show you how it works.

Say we render a list of talk components:

```
<talk-cmp *ngFor="let t of talks; let i=index" [talk]="t"
[index]="i"></talk-cmp>
```

This de-sugars it into:

```
<talk-cmp
  template="ngFor: let t of talks; let i=index"
  [talk]="t"
  [index]="i">
</talk-cmp>
```

which de-sugars into:

```
<template
  ngFor
  [ngForOf]="talks"
  let-t="$implicit"
  let-i="index">
    <talk-cmp [talk]="t" [index]="i"></talk-cmp>
</template>
```

It is important to understand what the * syntax expands into when you build your own directives that manipulate views. For instance, if you look at ngFor, you will see that it has the ngForOf property, but does not have the of property.

Let's recap

That's how Angular templates work. Let's see if they are analyzable and transformable, and if they provide the benefits I talked about at the beginning of this chapter.

Contrasting with Angular 1, there is a lot more the framework can tell about the template statically.

For example, regardless of what the component element is, Angular knows that name in [property1]="name" is a field read and name in property2="name" is a string literal. It also knows that the name property cannot be updated by the component: property bindings update from the parent to the child. Similarly, Angular can tell what variables are defined in the template by just looking at *ngFor. Finally, it can tell apart the static and dynamic parts in the template.

All of these allow us to reliably introspect and transform templates at compile time. That's a powerful feature, that, for instance, the Angular i18n support is built upon.

Having designed templates in this way, we also solved one of the biggest Angular 1 problems: IDE support. When using Angular 1, editors and IDEs had to do a lot of guessing to provide completion, refactoring, and navigation. Starting with Angular 2 IDEs no longer have to do any guessing. With the help of the @angular/language-service package they actually know what's available in the template. And, as a result, completion, refactoring, and navigation work reliably.

5
Dependency Injection

The idea behind dependency injection is very simple. If you have a component that depends on a service, you do not create that service yourself. Instead, you request one in the constructor, and the framework will provide you one. By doing so you can depend on interfaces rather than concrete types. This leads to more decoupled code, which enables testability, and other great things.

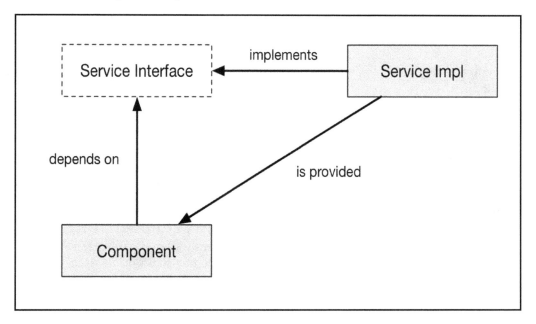

Angular comes with a dependency injection system. To see how it can be used, let's look at the following component, which renders a list of talks using the for directive:

```
@Component({
  selector: 'talks-cmp',
  template: `
    <h2>Talks:</h2>
    <talk *ngFor="let t of talks" [talk]="t"></talk>
  `
})
class TalksCmp {
  constructor() { //..get the data }
}
```

Let's mock up a simple service that will give us the data:

```
class TalksAppBackend {
  fetchTalks() {
    return [
      { name: 'Are we there yet?' },
      { name: 'The value of values' }
    ];
  }
}
```

How can you use this service? One approach is to create an instance of this service in our component.

```
class TalksCmp {
  constructor() {
    const backend = new TalksAppBackend();
    this.talks = backend.fetchTalks();
  }
}
```

This is fine for a demo app, but not good for real applications. In a real application, TalksAppBackend won't just return an array of objects, it will make HTTP requests to get the data. This means that the unit tests for this component will make real HTTP requests—not a great idea. This problem is caused by the fact that you have coupled TalksCmp to TalksAppBackend and its new operator.

You can solve this problem by injecting an instance of `TalksAppBackend` into the constructor, so you can easily replace it in tests, like this:

```
class TalksCmp {
  constructor(backend:TalksAppBackend) {
    this.talks = backend.fetchTalks();
  }
}
```

This tells Angular that `TalksCmp` depends on `TalksAppBackend`. Now, you need to tell Angular how to create an instance of `TalksAppBackend`.

Registering providers

To do that you need to register a provider, and there are two places where you can do it. One is in the component decorator.

```
@Component({
  selector: 'talks-cmp',
  template: `
    <h2>Talks:</h2>
    <talk *ngFor="let t of talks" [talk]="t"></talk>
  `,
  providers: [TalksAppBackend]
})
class TalksCmp {
  constructor(backend:TalksAppBackend) {
    this.talks = backend.fetchTalks();
  }
}
```

And the other one is in the module decorator.

```
@NgModule({
  declarations: [FormattedRatingPipe, WatchButtonCmp, \
    RateButtonCmp, TalkCmp, TalksCmp],
  exports: [TalksCmp],
  providers: [TalksAppBackend]
})
class TalksModule {}
```

What is the difference and which one should you prefer?

Generally, I recommend to register providers at the module level when they do not depend on the DOM, components, or directives. And only UI-related providers that have to be scoped to a particular component should be registered at the component level. Since `TalksAppBackend` has nothing to do with the UI, register it at the module level.

Injector tree

Now you know that the dependency injection configuration has two parts:

- **Registering providers**: How and where an object should be created.
- **Injecting dependencies**: What an object depends on.

And everything an object depends on (services, directives, and elements) is injected into its constructor. To make this work the framework builds a tree of injectors.

First, every DOM element with a component or a directive on it gets an injector. This injector contains the component instance, all the providers registered by the component, and a few "local" objects (for example, the element).

Second, when bootstrapping an NgModule, Angular creates an injector using the module and the providers defined there.

So the injector tree of the application will look like this:

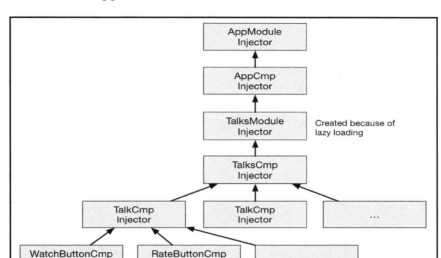

Resolution

And this is how the dependency resolution algorithm works:

```
// this is pseudocode.
let inj = this;
while (inj) {
  if (inj.has(requestedDependency)) {
    return inj.get(requestedDependency);
  } else {
    inj = inj.parent;
  }
}
throw new NoProviderError(requestedDependency);
```

When resolving the backend dependency of `TalksCmp`, Angular will start with the injector of the talks component itself. Then, if it is unsuccessful, it will climb up to the injector of the app component, and, finally, will move up to the injector created from `AppModule`. That is why, for `TalksAppBackend` to be resolved, you need to register it at `TalkCmp`, `AppCmp`, or `AppModule`.

Lazy loading

The setup gets more complex once you start using lazy-loading.

Lazy-loading a module is akin to bootstrapping a module in that it creates a new injector out of the module and plugs it into the injector tree. To see it in action, let's update our application to load the talks module lazily.

```
@NgModule({
  declarations: [AppCmp],
  providers: [RouterModule.forRoot([
    {path: 'talks', loadChildren: 'talks'}
  ])]
})
class AppModule {}

@NgModule({
  declarations: [FormattedRatingPipe, WatchButtonCmp, \
    RateButtonCmp, TalkCmp, TalksCmp],
  entryComponents: [TalksCmp],
  providers: [TalksAppBackend, RouteModule.forChild([
    {path: '', component: TalksCmp}
  ])]
})
class TalksModule {}
```

With this change, the injector tree will look as follows:

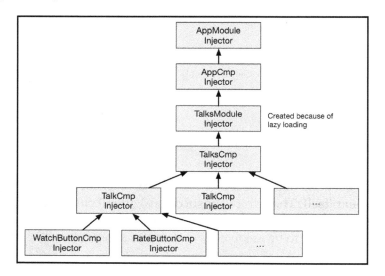

Getting injector

You can use `ngProbe` to poke at an injector associated with an element on the page. You can also see an element's injector when an exception is thrown.

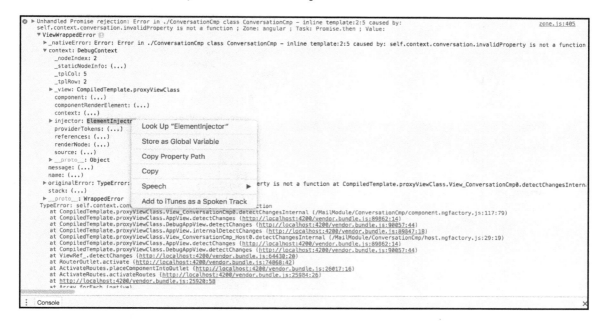

Right click on any of these objects to store them as a global variable, so you can interact with them in the console.

Visualizing injector tree

If you more of a visual person, use the Angular Augury (`https://augury.angular.io/`) chrome extension to inspect the component and injector trees.

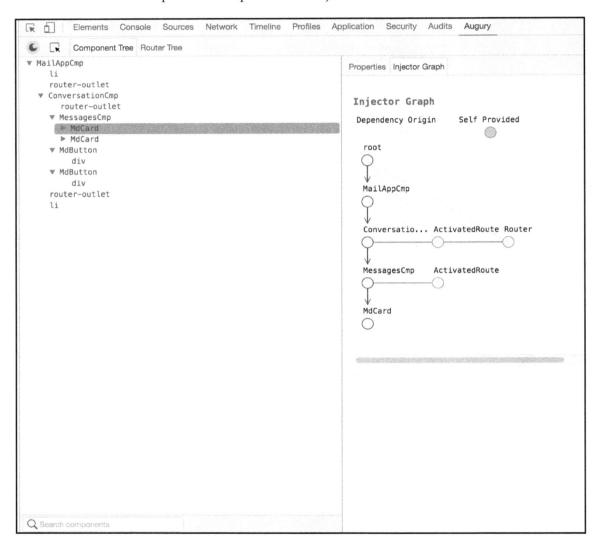

Advanced topics

Controlling visibility

You can be more specific where you want to get dependencies from. For instance, you can ask for another directive on the same element.

```
class CustomInputComponent {
  constructor(@Self() f: FormatterDirective) {}
}
```

Or you can ask for a directive in the same template, that is, you can only inject an ancestor directive from the same HTML file.

```
class CustomInputComponent {
  constructor(@Host() f: CustomForm) {}
}
```

Finally, you can ask to skip the current element, which can be handy for decorating existing providers or building up tree-like structures.

```
class SomeComponent {
  constructor(@SKipSelf() ancestor: SomeComponent) {}
}
```

Optional dependencies

To mark a dependency as optional, use the Optional decorator.

```
class Login {
  constructor(@Optional() service: LoginService) {}
}
```

More on registering providers

Passing a class into an array of providers is the same as using a provider with useClass, that is, the following two examples are identical:

```
@NgModule({
providers: [
    SomeClass
  ]
})
class MyModule {}
```

When useClass does not suffice, you can configure providers with useValue, useFactory, and useExisting.

```
@NgModule({
  providers: [
    { provide: 'one', useValue: 1},
    { provide: 'sameOne', useExisting: 'one'},
    { provide: 'sum', useFactory: (one, sameOne) => one + sameOne,\
      deps: ['one', 'sameOne']}
  ]
})
class MyModule {
  constructor(@Inject('sum') sum: number) {
    console.log("sum", sum);
  }
}
```

As you can see in the preceding code, we can use the @Inject decorator to configure dependencies when the type parameter does not match the provided token.

Aliasing

It's common for components and services to alias themselves.

```
@Component({
  selector: 'component-reexporting-itself',
  providers: [
    {provide: 'alias', useExisting: forwardRef(() =>\
      ComponentReexportingItself)}
  ]
})
class ComponentReexportingItself {}
```

Now we can use both `@Inject(ComponentReexportingItself)` and
`@Inject('alias')` to inject this component.

Overrides

The providers of the imported modules are merged with the target module's providers, left to right, that is, if multiple imported modules define the same provider, the last one wins.

```
@NgModule({
  providers: [
    {provide: 'token', useValue: 'A'}
  ]
})
class ModuleA {}

@NgModule({
  providers: [
    {provide: 'token', useValue: 'B'}
  ]
})
class ModuleB {}

@NgModule({
  imports: [ModuleA, ModuleB]
})
class ModuleC {
  constructor(@Inject('token') t: string) {
    console.log(t); // will print 'B'
  }
}
```

The preceding example will print B. If we change ModuleC to have its own token provider, that one will be used, and the example will print C.

```
@NgModule({
  imports: [ModuleA, ModuleB],
  providers: [
    {provide: 'token', useValue: 'C'}
  ]
})
class ModuleC {
  constructor(@Inject('token') t: string) {
    console.log(t); // will print 'C'
  }
}
```

Let's recap

- Dependency injection is a key component of Angular
- You can configure dependency injection at the component or module level
- Dependency injection allows us to depend on interfaces rather than concrete types
- This results in more decoupled code
- This improves testability

6
Change Detection

Two phases

Angular separates updating the application model and reflecting the state of the model in the view into two distinct phases. The developer is responsible for updating the application model. Angular via bindings, by means of change detection, is responsible for reflecting the state of the model in the view. The framework does it automatically on every VM turn.

Event bindings, which can be added using the ( ) syntax, can be used to capture a browser event or component output to execute some function on a component or a directive. So they often trigger the first phase.

Property bindings, which can be added using the [ ] syntax, should be used only for reflecting the state of the model in the view.

As we have learned, an Angular application consists of nested components, so it will always have a component tree. Let's say for this app it looks as follows:

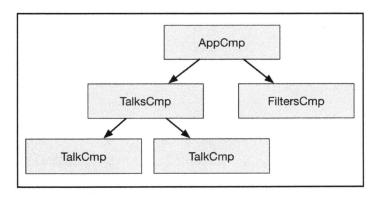

Next, define the application model that will store the state of our application.

```
{
    "filters": {"speakers": "Rich Hickey"},
    "talks": [
        {
            "id":898,
            "title": "Are we there yet",
            "speaker": "Rich Hickey",
            "yourRating":null,
            "rating": 9.1
        },
    ]
}
```

Now, imagine an event changing the model. Let's say I watched the talk *Are we there yet*, I really liked it, and I decided to give it 9.9.

The following code snippet shows one way to do it. The `handleRate` function is called, via an event binding, when the user rates a talk.

```
Component({
    selector: 'talk',
    template: `
        {{talk.title}} {{talk.speaker}}
        {{talk.rating | formatRating}}
        <watch-button [talk]="talk"></watch-button>
        <rate-button [talk]="talk" (rate)="handleRate($event)">\
        </rate-button>
        `
})
class TalkCmp {
    @Input() talk:Talk;

    constructor(private app: App){}

    handleRate(newRating: number) {
        this.app.rateTalk(this.talk, newRating);
    }
}

@Component({
    selector: 'talks',
    template: `
        <h2>Talks:</h2>
        <talk *ngFor="let t of app.talks" [talk]="t"></talk>
        `
})
```

```
class TalksCmp {
  constructor(public app: App) {}
}

// contains the business logic
class App {
  talks: Talk[] = [];

  rateTalk(talk: Talk, rating: number){
    // model is immutable, so we have to build a new model object
    // constructing a new talk instance with an updated rating
    const updatedTalk = updateRecord(talk, {rating});

    // constructing a new collection instance
    this.talks = updateArray(this.talks, updatedTalk);
  }
}
```

In this example, we do not mutate the `talk`, and instead create a new array of new talks every time a change happens, which results in a few good properties. But it is worth noting that Angular doesn't require us to use immutable objects, and we could just as easily write something like `talk.rating = newRating`.

All right, after `rateTalk` executes, the updated model will look like this:

```
{
  "filters": {"speakers": "Rich Hickey"},
  "talks": [
    {
      "id":898,
      "title": "Are we there yet",
      "speaker": "Rich Hickey",
      "yourRating": 9.9,
      "rating": 9.1
    },
  ]
}
```

At this point, nothing has changed in the view. Only the model has been updated.

Next, at the end of the VM turn, change detection kicks in to propagate changes in the view.

First, change detection goes through every component in the component tree to check if the model it depends on changed. And if it did, it will update the component. In this example, the first talk component gets updated:

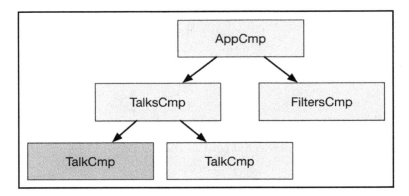

Then, the framework updates the DOM. In our example, the rate button gets disabled because we cannot rate the same talk twice.

Note, the framework has used **change detection** and **property bindings** to execute this phase.

In our example, we are using shared state and immutable data. But even if we used local state and mutable data, it would not change the property that the application model update and the view state propagation are separated.

Why?

Now, when we have understood how we had separated the two phases, let's talk about why we did it.

Predictability

First, using change detection only for updating the view state limits the number of places where the application model can be changed. In this example, it can happen only in the rateTalk function. A watcher cannot "automagically" update it. This makes ensuring invariants easier, which makes code easier to troubleshoot and refactor.

Second, it helps us understand the view state propagation. Consider what we can say about the talk component just by looking at it in isolation. Since we use immutable data, we know that as long as we do not do talk= in the Talk component, the only way to change what the component displays is by updating the input. These are strong guarantees that allow us to think about this component in isolation.

Finally, by explicitly stating what the application and the framework are responsible for, we can set different constraints on each part. For instance, it is natural to have cycles in the application model. So the framework should support it. On the other hand, HTML forces components to form a tree structure. We can take advantage of this and make the system more predictable.

 Starting with Angular 2 it gets easier to think about components because the framework limits the number of ways it can modify the components, and those modifications are predictable.

Performance

The major benefit of the separation is that it allows us to constrain the view state propagation. This makes the system more predictable, but it also makes it a lot more performant. For example, the fact that the change detection graph in Angular can be modeled as a tree allowed us to get rid of digest TTL (multiple digest runs until no changes occur). Now the system gets stable after a single pass.

How does Angular enforce It?

What happens if I try to break the separation? What if I try to change the application model inside a setter that is invoked by the change detection system?

Angular tries to make sure that the setter we define for our component only updates the view state of this component or its children and not the application model. To do that Angular will check all bindings twice in the developer mode. First time to propagate changes, and second time to make sure there are no changes. If it finds a change during the second pass, it means that one of our setters updated the application model, the framework will throw an exception, pointing at the place where the violation happened.

Content and view children

Earlier I said "change detection goes through every component in the component tree to check if the model it depends on changed" without saying much about how the framework does it. In what order does it do it? Understanding this is crucial, and that's what I'm going to cover in this section.

There are two types of children a component can have: **content children** and **view children**. To understand the difference between them, let's look at the following example:

```
@Component({
  selector: 'tab',
  template: `...`
})
class TabCmp {
}

@Component({
  selector: 'tabs',
  template: `
    Number of tabs: {{tabs.length}}
    <div>
      <ng-content></ng-content>
    </div>
    <div>
      <button (click)="selectPrev()">Prev</button>
      <button (click)="selectNext()">Next</button>
    </div>
  `
})
class TabsCmp {
  @ContentChildren(TabCmp) tabs: QueryList<Tab>;
}

@Component({
  template: `
    <tabs>
      <tab ></tab>
      <tab ></tab>
      <tab ></tab>
    </tabs>
  `
})
class CmpUsingTabs {
}
```

The content children of the `tabs` component are the three `tab` components. The user of the `tabs` component provided those. The previous and next buttons are the view children of the `tabs` component. The author of the `tabs` component provided those.

This is the order in which Angular will check the bindings:

- It will check the bindings of the `tabs` component first, of which there are none
- It will check the three `tab` components, the content children of the `tabs` component
- It will check the template of the tabs component

ChangeDetectionStrategy.OnPush

If we use mutable objects that are shared among multiple components, Angular cannot know about when those components can be affected. A component can affect any other components in the system. That is why, by default, Angular does not make any assumptions about what a component depends upon. So it has be conservative and check every template of every component on every browser event. Since the framework has to do it for every component, it might become a performance problem even though the change detection in the new versions of Angular got way faster.

If our model application state uses immutable objects, like in the preceding example, we can tell a lot more about when the talk component can change. The component can change if and only if any of its inputs changes. And we can communicate it to Angular by setting the change detection strategy to `OnPush`.

```
Component({
  selector: 'talk',
  template: `
    {{talk.title}} {{talk.speaker}}
    {{talk.rating | formatRating}}
    <watch-button [talk]="talk"></watch-button>
    <rate-button [talk]="talk" (rate)="handleRate($event)">\
    </rate-button>
  `,
  changeDetection: ChangeDetectionStrategy.OnPush
})
class TalkCmp {
  //...
}
```

Using this change-detection strategy restricts when Angular has to check for updates from "any time something might change" to "only when this component's inputs have changed". As a result, the framework can be a lot more efficient about detecting changes in `TalkCmp`. If no inputs change, no need to check the component's template. In addition to depending on immutable inputs `OnPush` components can also have local mutable state.

Let's recap

- Angular separates updating the application model and updating the view.
- Event bindings are used to update the application model.
- Change detection uses property bindings to update the view. Updating the view is unidirectional and top-down. This makes the system more predictable and performant.
- We make the system more efficient by using the `OnPush` change detection strategy for the components that depend on immutable input and only have local mutable state.

7
Forms

Web applications heavily rely on forms. In many ways Angular is so successful because two-way bindings and `ng-model` made creating dynamic forms easy.

Although very flexible, the AngularJS 1.x approach has some issues: the data flow in complex user interactions is hard to understand and debug.

Angular 2+ builds up on the ideas from AngularJS 1.x: it preserves the ease of creating dynamic forms, but avoids the issues making data flow hard to understand.

In this chapter we will look at how form handling (or input handling) works in Angular.

Two modules

In AngularJS 1.x, the `ng-model` directive was baked into the core framework. This is no longer the case. The `@angular/core` package doesn't contain a form-handling library. It only provides the key primitives we can use to build one.

Of course, making everyone to build their own would not be practical. And that's why the Angular team built the `@angular/forms` package with two modules: `FormsModule` and `ReactiveFormsModule`.

`FormsModule` implements AngularJS-style form handling. We create a form by placing directives in the template. We then use data bindings to get data in and out of that form.

`ReactiveFormsModule` is another take on handling input, where we define a form in the component class and just bind it to elements in the template. We tend to use reactive programming to get data in and out of the form, hence the name "reactive".

At first glance, these two modules seem very different. But once we understand the underlying mechanisms, we will see how much they have in common. In addition, it will give us an idea of how to build our own form-handling module if needed.

High-level overview

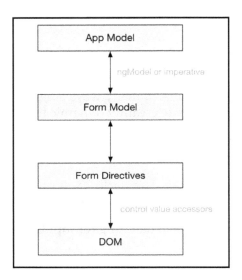

App model

The app model is an object provided by the application developer. It can be a JSON object fetched from the server, or some object constructed on the client side. Angular doesn't make any assumptions about it.

Form model

The form model is a UI-independent representation of a form. It consists of three building blocks: `FormControl`, `FormGroup`, and `FormArray`. We will look at the form model in detail later in this chapter. Both `FormsModule` and `ReactiveFormsModule` use this model.

Form directives

These are the directives connecting the form model to the DOM (for example, NgModel). `FormsModule` and `ReactiveFormsModule` provide different sets of these directives.

DOM

These are ours inputs, checkboxes, and radio buttons.

Form model

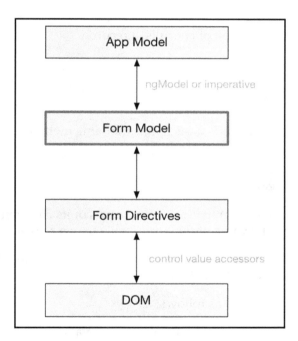

To make form handling less UI-dependent, `@angular/forms` provides a set of primitives for modelling forms: `FormControl`, `FormGroup`, and `FormArray`.

FormControl

FormControl is an indivisible part of the form, an atom. It usually corresponds to a simple UI element, such as an input.

```
const c = new FormControl('Init Value', Validators.required);
```

A FormControl has a value, status, and a map of errors:

```
expect(c.value).toEqual('Init Value');
expect(c.errors).toEqual(null); //null means 'no errors'
expect(c.status).toEqual('VALID');
```

FormGroup

FormGroup is a fixed-size collection of controls, a record.

```
const c = new FormGroup({
  login: new FormControl(''),
  password: new FormControl('', Validators.required)
});
```

A FormGroup is itself a control, and, as such, has the same methods as FormControl.

```
expect(c.value).toEqual({login: '', password: ''});
expect(c.errors).toEqual(null);
expect(c.status).toEqual('INVALID');
```

The value of a group is just an aggregation of the values of its children. Any time the value of a child control changes, the value of the group will change as well.

In opposite to the value, the form group doesn't aggregate the errors of its children. It has its own validators and its own collection of errors.

The status of a group is calculated as follows:

- If one of its children is invalid, the group is invalid
- If all of its children are valid, but the group itself has errors, the group is invalid
- If all of its children are valid, and the group has no errors, the group is valid

Since `FormGroup` acts like a control, we can nest them in arbitrary ways.

```
const c = new FormGroup({
  login: new FormControl(''),
  passwords: new FormGroup({
    password: new FormControl(''),
    passwordConfirmation: new FormControl('')
  })
});
```

FormArray

Whereas `FormGroup` is a collection of different control types of fixed length, `FormArray` is a collection of the same control type of a variable length.

```
const c = new FormArray([
  new FormControl('one', Validators.required),
  new FormControl('two', Validators.required)
]);
```

All the considerations regarding `value`, `status`, and `errors` of `FormGroup` apply here as well.

Updating form model

```
const c = new FormGroup({
  login: new FormControl(''),
  passwords: new FormGroup({
    password: new FormControl(''),
    passwordConfirmation: new FormControl('')
  }),
  notes: new FormArray([
    new FormControl('Buy wine'),
    new FormControl('Buy cheese')
  ])
});
```

There are two ways to update the value of a form: `setValue` and `patchValue`:

- The `setValue` method is strict and requires the value to match the structure of the form.

```
c.setValue({
  login: 'newLogin',
  password: {
    password: 'newPassword',
    passwordConfirmation: 'newPassword'
  },
  notes: [
    'buy wine!!!',
    'buy cheese!!!'
  ]
});
```

  If we try to set the value of a control that doesn't exist, or if we exclude the value of a control, `setValue` will fail.

- The `patchValue` method works as `setValue` except that it doesn't throw an error when the value is a superset or a subset of the form.

```
c.patchValue({
  login: 'newLogin',
  password: {
    passwordConfirmation: 'newPassword'
  },
  somethingEntirelyDifferent: true
});
```

By default updating a control will update its parents. We can prevent the change from propagating through the parents by passing `onlySelf: true`:

```
c.setValue('newLogin', {onlySelf: true});
```

Disabling form model

```
const c = new FormGroup({
  login: new FormControl(''),
  password: new FormControl('', Validators.required),
  acceptTerms: new FormControl(null)
});
const acceptTerms = c.get('acceptTerms');
acceptTerms.disable();

expect(c.value).toEqual({login: '', password: ''});
```

This exempts `acceptTerms` validation checks and excludes it from the aggregate value of any parent. Its status gets set to `DISABLED`.

Async validations

The `required` validator we have used throughout the chapter is synchronous. The moment we set value, the moment the control goes into the `VALID` or `INVALID` state. Some validations, however, have to be asynchronous. A good example is the uniqueness of the login.

```
const login = new FormControl('', null, uniqLoginValidator); \
// null is sync validator
login.setValue('john66');
```

This will set the status of the control and its parents to `PENDING`. And, once the promise returned by `uniqLoginValidator` resolves, the status will be set to either `INVALID` or `VALID`.

In addition to declarative validators, we can always set the errors on the control imperatively.

```
login.setErrors({uniq: false});
```

Composing validators

A **validator** is just a function that takes a control and returns a map of errors.

```
class Validators {
  static required(control): {[key: string]: any} {
    return isEmptyInputValue(control.value) ? {'required': true} :
    null;
  }
}
```

The `value` doesn't have to be a Boolean. We can provide extra information to create a more meaningful error message.

```
class Validators {
  static minLength(minLength: number): ValidatorFn {
    return (control): {[key: string]: any} => {
      const length: number = control.value ? \
      control.value.length : 0;
      return length < minLength ?
          {'minlength': {'requiredLength': minLength, \
          'actualLength': length}} : null;
    };
  }
}
```

Since the return value of a validator is a "map", and not a single value, it's easy to compose multiple validators into one.

```
const between3And30: ValidatorFn = Validators.compose([
  Validators.minLength(3),
  Validators.maxLength(30)
]);
```

The provided `compose` function will execute all the validators and merge the errors. We can, of course, implement our own `compose` function that, for instance, will execute validators until the first failure.

Listening to changes

Any time a control updates, it will emit the value.

```
const login = new FormControl('');
const password = new FormControl('', Validators.required);
const c = new FormGroup({login, password});

login.valueChanges.subscribe(c => console.log("login value updates to",
c));
login.statusChanges.subscribe(c => console.log("login status updates to",
c));

password.valueChanges.subscribe(c => console.log("password value updates
to", c));
password.statusChanges.subscribe(c => console.log("password status updates
to", c));

c.valueChanges.subscribe(c => console.log("form value updates to", c));
c.statusChanges.subscribe(c => console.log("form status updates to", c));

login.setValue('newLogin');
password.setValue('newPassword');

// will print:
// login value updates to 'newLogin'
// form value updates to {login: 'newLogin', password: ''}
// password value updates to 'newPassword'
// password status updates to 'VALID'
// form value updates to {login: 'newLogin', password:\ 'newPassword'}
// form status updates to 'VALID'
```

As you can see the value of the form has been updated twice. We can prevent this by setting the value on the form itself.

```
const c = new FormGroup({login, password});
c.setValue({login: 'newLogin', password: 'newPassword'});

// will print:
// login value updates to 'newLogin'
// password value updates to 'newPassword'
// password status updates to 'VALID'
// form value updates to {login: 'newLogin', password: 'newPassword'}
// form status updates to 'VALID'
```

We can also prevent the events from being emitted altogether by passing `emitEvent: false`.

Power of RxJS

Since `valueChanges` and `statusChanges` are RxJS observables, we can use the rich set of RxJS combinators to implement powerful user interactions in a just a few lines of code.

Why form model?

The form model is a UI-independent way to represent user input comprising simple controls (`FormControl`) and their combinations (`FormGroup` and `FormArray`), where:

- Each control has a value
- Each control has a status
- Each control has validators and errors
- Each control can be disabled
- Each control emits events

Having this model has the following advantages:

- Form handling is a complex problem. Splitting it into UI-independent and UI-dependent parts makes them easier to manage.
- We can test form handling without rendering UI.
- Having the form model makes reactive forms possible (see the following sections).

Form directives

Abstractly describing input is all well and good, but at some point we will need to connect it to the UI.

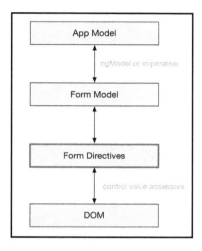

`@angular/forms` provides two modules that do that: `FormsModule` and `ReactiveFormsModule`.

ReactiveFormsModule

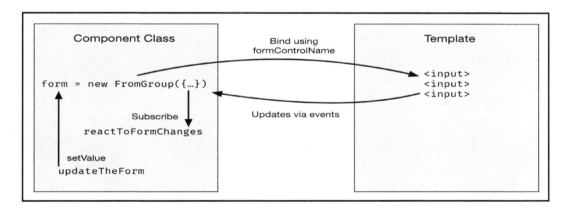

ReactiveFormsModule is simpler to understand and explain than FormsModule. That's why I will cover it first.

```
@Component({
selector: 'filters-cmp',
template: `
    <div [formGroup]="filters">
      <input formControlName="title" placeholder="Title">
      <input formControlName="speaker" placeholder="Speaker">
      <input type="checkbox" formControlName="highRating">
      High Rating
    </div>
`
})
export class FiltersCmp {
  filters = new FormGroup({
    speaker: new FormControl(),
    title: new FormControl(),
    highRating: new FormControl(false),
  });

  constructor(app: App) {
    this.filters.valueChanges.debounceTime(200).\
    subscribe((value) => {
      app.applyFilters(value);
    });
  }
}

@NgModule({
  imports: [
    ReactiveFormsModule
  ],
  declarations: [
    FiltersCmp
  ]
})
class AppModule {}
```

There are a few things here to note.

First, we import ReactiveFormsModule, which provides, among others, the formGroup and formControlName directives.

Second, we manually construct a form model.

```
filters = new FormGroup({
speaker: new FormControl(),
title: new FormControl(),
highRating: new FormControl(false),
});
```

Third, we bind the constructed form to the div using formGroup. Then we use formControlName to bind the title, speaker, and highRating to the three inputs. The Name suffix indicates that we need to pass the name of a field of the containing group.

When using ReactiveFormsModule we are responsible for creating the form model. We use the directives merely to bind the form to elements in the UI.

Then we use the constructed form model directly to synchronize it with the client model or trigger events. And we often do it by subscribing to the valueChanges and statusChanges observables.

FormsModule

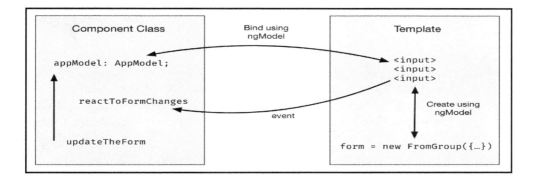

`FormsModule` implements AngularJS-style forms.

```
@Component({
selector: 'filters-cmp',
template: `
    <form (submit)="applyFilters()">
      <input [(ngModel)]="speaker" name="speaker" placeholder="Speaker">
      <input [(ngModel)]="title" name="title" placeholder="Title">
      <input [(ngModel)]="highRating" name="highRating"
      type="checkbox">High Rating
    </form>
    `
})
export class FiltersCmp {
  speaker: string;
  title: string;
  highRating: boolean;

  constructor(private app: App) {}

  applyFilters() {
    this.app.applyFilters({speaker, title, highRating});
  }
}

@NgModule({
  imports: [
    FormsModule
  ],
  declarations: [
    FiltersCmp
  ]
})
class AppModule {}
```

This is similar to AngularJS 1.x. We use the `[()]` syntax (see `Chapter 6`, *Change Detection*) to bind the `speaker`, `title`, and `highRating` properties of the filters component to the three inputs. We then invoke the `applyFilters` method when the user submits the form.

Even though it's not seen in the example, the following form group still gets created:

```
filters = new FormGroup({
  speaker: new FormControl(),
  title: new FormControl(),
  highRating: new FormControl(false),
});
```

The difference is that it does not get created by the application developer, but by the NgModel and NgForm directives.

- The NgForm directive gets instantiated at <form (submit)="applyFilters()">. This directive creates an empty FormGroup.

- The NgModel directive gets instantiated at <input [(ngModel)]="speaker" name="speaker" placeholder="Speaker">. This directive creates a FormControl and adds it to the FormGroup created by the encompassing NgForm.

How is it possible?

If you have read the chapter on change detection carefully, you probably wonder how this works. Shouldn't the following fail?

```
@Component({
selector: 'filters-cmp',
template: `
    {{f.controls.speaker == null}}

    <form #f="ngForm" (submit)="applyFilters()">
      <input ngModel name="speaker" placeholder="Speaker">
      <input ngModel name="title" placeholder="Title">
      <input ngModel name="highRating" type="checkbox">High Rating
    </form>
`
})
export class FiltersCmp {
  //...
}
```

If NgModel and NgForm were implemented naively, the {{f.controls.speaker == null}} binding would evaluate to true the first time, when the group is empty, and will evaluate to false once NgModels add their form controls to the group. This change from true to false will happen within a change detection run, which, in opposite to AngularJS 1.x, is disallowed in Angular 2+. The value of a binding can change only between change detection runs.

To make it work, NgModel doesn't add a form control synchronously—it does it in a microtask. In the preceding example, the three ngModels will schedule three microtasks to add the speaker, title, and highRating controls.

During the first change detection run, the form will always be empty and {{f.controls.speaker == null}} will always evaluate to true. Then, after the three microtasks, Angular will run change detection again, and {{f.controls.speaker == null}} will evaluate to false.

This is how we can preserve all the guarantees of Angular 2+ and still make the API feel AngularJS-like.

Accessing form model when using FormsModule

We can still access the form model by either querying for the NgForm directive or by referencing it in the template.

```
@Component({
selector: 'filters-cmp',
template: `
    <form   (submit)="applyFilters()">
      <input ngModel name="speaker" placeholder="Speaker">
      <input ngModel name="title" placeholder="Title">
      <input ngModel name="highRating" type="checkbox">High Rating
    </form>
    `
})
export class FiltersCmp {
  @ViewChild(NgForm) ngForm: NgForm;

  constructor(private app: App) {}

  applyFilters() {
    this.app.applyFiltes(ngForm.form.value);
  }
}
```

```
@Component({
selector: 'filters-cmp',
template: `
    <form  #f="ngForm" (submit)="applyFilters(f.form)">
        <input ngModel name="speaker" placeholder="Speaker">
        <input ngModel name="title" placeholder="Title">
        <input ngModel name="highRating" type="checkbox">High Rating
    </form>
    `
})
export class FiltersCmp {
  constructor(private app: App) {}

  applyFilters(g: FormGroup) {
    this.app.applyFiltes(g.value);
  }
}
```

Once we get the model, we can interact with it imperatively or subscribe to its observables.

The DOM

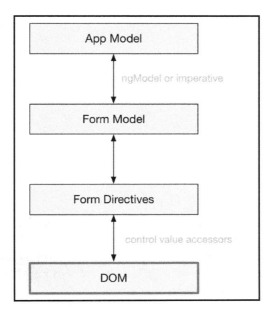

The ngModel, ngControlName, and other form directives bind the form model to UI elements, which are often native to the platform (for example, <input>), but they do not have to be. For instance, NgModel can be applied to an Angular component.

```
<md-input [(ngModel)]="speaker" name="speaker" placeholder="Speaker">
```

A ControlValueAccessor is a directive that acts like a adapter connecting a UI element to NgModel. It knows how to read and write to the native UI-element.

The @angular/forms package comes with value accessors for all built-in UI elements (input, textarea, so on). But if we want to apply an NgModel to a custom element or an Angular component, we will have to provide a value accessor for it ourselves.

```
@Component({
  selector: 'custom-input',
  providers: [
    {
      provide: NG_VALUE_ACCESSOR,
      useExisting: forwardRef(() => CustomInputCmp),
      multi: true
    }
  ]
})
class CustomInputCmp implements ControlValueAccessor {
  //...
}
```

Wrapping up

Form handling is a complex problem. One of the main reasons AngularJS got so successful is that two-way bindings and ng-model provided a good solution for it. But there were some downsides, mainly complex forms built with ng-model made the data flow of the application hard to follow and debug. Angular 2+ builds up on the ideas from Angular 1, but avoids its problems.

NgModel and friends are no longer part of the core framework. The @angular/core package only contains the primitives we can use to build a form-handling module. Instead, Angular has a separate package—@angular/forms—that comes with FormsModule and ReactiveFormsModule that provide two different styles of handling user input.

Both the modules depend on the form model consisting of `FormControl`, `FormGroup`, and `FormArray`. Having this UI-independent model, we can model and test input handling without rendering any components.

Finally, `@angular/forms` comes with a set of directives to handle build-in UI elements (such as `<input>`), but we can provide our own.

8
Testing

One of the design goals of Angular is to make testing easy. That's why the framework relies on dependency injection, separates the user code from the framework code, and comes with a set of tools for writing and running tests. In this chapter I will look at four ways to test Angular components: isolated tests, shallow tests, integration tests, and protractor tests.

Isolated tests

It is often useful to test complex components without rendering them. To see how it can be done, let's write a test for the following component:

```
@Component({
  selector: 'filters-cmp',
  templateUrl: './filters.component.html',
  styleUrls: ['./filters.component.css']
})
export class FiltersCmp {
  @Output() change = new EventEmitter();

  filters = new FormGroup({
    speaker: new FormControl(),
    title: new FormControl(),
    highRating: new FormControl(false),
  });

  constructor(@Inject('createFiltersObject') createFilters: Function) {
    this.filters.valueChanges.debounceTime(200).\
    subscribe((value) => {
      this.change.next(createFilters(value));
    });
  }
}
```

Following is the code for `filters.component.html`:

```html
<div [formGroup]="filters">
  <md-input-container>
    <input md-input formControlName="title" placeholder="Title">
  </md-input-container>

  <md-input-container>
    <input md-input formControlName="speaker" placeholder="Speaker">
  </md-input-container>

  <md-checkbox formControlName="highRating">
    High Rating
  </md-checkbox>
</div>
```

There a few things in this example worth noting:

- We are using reactive forms in the template of this component. This require us to manually create a form object in the component class, which has a nice consequence: we can test input handling without rendering the template.

- We listen to all the form changes, debounce them using the RxJS `debounceTime` operator, and then emit a change event.

- Finally, we inject a function to create a filters object out of the form.

Now, let's look at the test:

```
describe('FiltersCmp', () => {
  describe("when filters change", () => {
    it('should fire a change event after 200 millis', \
    fakeAsync(() => {
      const component = new FiltersCmp((v) => v);

      const events = [];
      component.change.subscribe(v => events.push(v));

      component.filters.controls['title'].setValue('N');
      setTimeout(() => {\
      component.filters.controls['title'].setValue('Ne'); }, 150);
      setTimeout(() => {\
      component.filters.controls['title'].setValue('New'); }, 200);

      expect(events).toEqual([]);
      tick(1000);
```

```
      // only one item because of debouncing
      expect(events).toEqual([
        {title: 'New', speaker: null, highRating: false}
      ]);

      component.filters.controls['title'].setValue('New!');

      tick(1000);
      expect(events).toEqual([
        {title: 'New', speaker: null, highRating: false},
        {title: 'New!', speaker: null, highRating: false}
      ]);
    }));
  });
});
```

As you can see, testing Angular components in isolation is no different from testing any other JavaScript object. We do not use any Angular UI-specific utilities. We, however, use `fakeAsync`. This is a utility provided by Zone.js and using it we can control time, which is handy for testing the debouncing. Also, this test does not exercise the template of this component. The template might as well be empty—the test will still pass.

Shallow testing

Testing component classes without rendering their templates works in certain scenarios, but not in all of them. Sometimes we can write a meaningful test only if we render a component's template. We can do that and still keep the test isolated. We just need to render the template without rendering the component's children. This is what is colloquially known as **shallow testing**.

Let's see this approach in action.

```
@Component({
  selector: 'talks-cmp',
  template: '<talk-cmp *ngFor="let t of talks" [talk]="t"></talk-cmp>'
})
export class TalksCmp {
  @Input() talks: Talk[];
}
```

This component simply renders a collection of `TalkCmp`.

Now let's look at its test.

```
import { async, ComponentFixture, TestBed } from '@angular/core/testing';
import { By } from '@angular/platform-browser';
import { DebugElement, NO_ERRORS_SCHEMA } from '@angular/core';

import { TalksCmp } from './talks.component';

describe('TalksCmp', () => {
  let component: TalksCmp;
  let fixture: ComponentFixture<TalksCmp>;

  beforeEach(async(() => {
    TestBed.configureTestingModule({
      declarations: [TalksCmp],
      schemas: [NO_ERRORS_SCHEMA]
    })
    .compileComponents();
  }));

  beforeEach(() => {
    fixture = TestBed.createComponent(TalksCmp);
    component = fixture.componentInstance;
    fixture.detectChanges();
  });

  it('should render a list of talks', () => {
    component.talks = <any>[
      { title: 'Are we there yet?' },
      { title: 'The Value of Values' }
    ];
    fixture.detectChanges();

    const s = fixture.debugElement.nativeElement;
    const ts = s.querySelectorAll("talk-cmp");

    expect(ts.length).toEqual(2);
    expect(ts[0].talk.title).toEqual('Are we there yet?');
    expect(ts[1].talk.title).toEqual('The Value of Values');
  });
});
```

First, look at how we configured our testing module. We only declared `TalksCmp`, nothing else. This means that all the elements in the template will be treated as simple DOM nodes, and only common directives (for example, `ngIf` and `ngFor`) will be applied. This is exactly what we want. Second, passing `NO_ERRORS_SCHEMA` tells the compiler not to error on unknown elements and attributes, which is what we need for shallow tests. The result will create a list of talk-cmp DOM elements, which we inspected in the test. No instances of `TalkCmp` were created.

Integration testing

We can also write an integration test that will exercise the whole application.

```
import {TestBed, async, ComponentFixture, inject} from
'@angular/core/testing';
import {AppCmp} from './app.component';
import {AppModule} from './app.module';
import {App} from "./app";

describe('AppCmp', () => {
  let component: AppCmp;
  let fixture: ComponentFixture<AppCmp>;
  let el: Element;

  beforeEach(async(() => {
    TestBed.configureTestingModule({
      imports: [AppModule]
    });
    TestBed.compileComponents();
  }));

  beforeEach(() => {
    fixture = TestBed.createComponent(AppCmp);
    component = fixture.componentInstance;
    fixture.detectChanges();
    el = fixture.debugElement.nativeElement;
  });

  it('should filter talks by title', async(inject([App], \
    (app: App) => {
    app.model.talks = [
      {
        "id": 1,
        "title": "Are we there yet?",
        "speaker": "Rich Hickey",
        "yourRating": null,
```

```
        "rating": 9.0
      },
      {
        "id": 2,
        "title": "The Value of Values",
        "speaker": "Rich Hickey",
        "yourRating": null,
        "rating": 8.0
      },
    ];
    fixture.detectChanges();

    expect(el.innerHTML).toContain("Are we there yet?");
    expect(el.innerHTML).toContain("The Value of Values");

    component.handleFiltersChange({
      title: 'we',
      speaker: null,
      minRating: 0
    });
    fixture.detectChanges();

    expect(el.innerHTML).toContain("Are we there yet?");
    expect(el.innerHTML).not.toContain("The Value of Values");
  }))));
});
```

Note here we are importing `AppModule`, which means that Angular will create all the registered provides and will compile all the registered components. The test itself is self explanatory.

Even though both the shallow and integration tests render components, these tests are very different in nature. In the shallow test we mock up every single dependency of a component, and we do not render any of the component's children. The goal is to exercise one slice of the component tree in isolation. In the integration tests we mock up only platform dependencies (for example, location), and we use production code for the rest. Shallow tests are isolated, and, as a result, can be used to drive the design of our components. Integration tests are only used to check the correctness.

Protractor tests

Finally, we can always write a protractor test exercising the whole application.

```
import {browser, element, by} from 'protractor';

export class TalksAppPage {
  navigateTo() {
    return browser.get('/');
  }

  getTitleInput() {
    return element(by.css('input[formcontrolname=title]'));
  }

  getTalks() {
    return element.all(by.css('talk-cmp'));
  }

  getTalkText(index: number) {
    return this.getTalks().get(index).geText();
  }
}

describe('e2e tests', function() {
  let page: TalksAppPage;

  beforeEach(() => {
    page = new TalksAppPage();
  });

  it('should filter talks by title', () => {
    page.navigateTo();

    const title = page.getTitleInput();
    title.sendKeys("Are we there");

    expect(page.getTalks().count()).toEqual(1);
    expect(page.getTalkText(0)).toContain("Are we there yet?");
  });
});
```

First, we created a page object, which is a good practice for making tests more domain-centric, so they talk more about user stories and not the DOM. Second, we wrote a protractor test verifying that filtering by title works.

Both protractor tests and integration tests (as defined in the preceding code), solve the same problem—they verify correctness, that is, they verify that a particular use case have been implemented. Which ones should we use? I tend to test most of the behavior using integration tests, and use protractor only for a few smoke tests, but it is highly dependent on the culture of the team.

Let's recap

In this chapter we looked at four ways to test Angular components: isolated tests, shallow tests, integration tests, and protractor tests. Each of them have their time and place: isolated tests are a great way to test drive your components and test complex logic. Shallow tests are isolated tests on steroids, and they should be used when writing a meaningful test requires to render a component's template. Finally, integration and protractor tests verify that a group of components and services (i.e., the application) work together.

9
Reactive Programming in Angular

Reactive programming in the core framework

An Angular application is a reactive system. The user clicks on a button, the application reacts to this event and updates the model. The model gets updated, the application propagates the changes through the component tree.

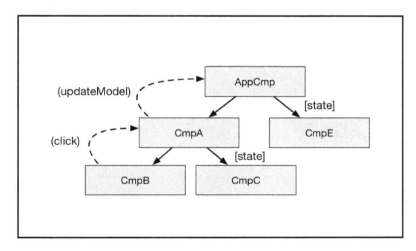

Angular implements these two arrows very differently. Let's explore why.

Events and state

To understand why Angular uses two very different ways of reactive programming, we need to look at the differences between events and the state.

We often talk about events or event streams when discussing reactivity. Event streams are an important category of reactive objects, but so is state. So let's compare their properties.

Events are discrete and cannot be skipped. Every single event matters, including the order in which the events are emitted. The "most recent event" is not a special thing we care about. Finally, very rarely are events directly displayed to the user.

State, on the other hand, is continuous, that is, it is defined at any point in time. We usually do not care about how many times it gets updated—only the most recent value matters. The state is often displayed or has a meaningful serialization form.

Say the conference application we use in this book has a **Load More** button, clicking on which loads more items and adds them to the list. Using this button and mouse click events we can change the content of the list. Clicking on the button increases the number of items. The number of clicks matters. And we cannot skip any of them, as it would change the content of the list. Finally, we will never have to examine the last click event or display it to the user.

The list itself, on the other hand, is the state. We only care about its latest value, not about how many times it was updated.

Definition

Event streams are sequences of values produced over a period of time. And the state is a single value that varies over time.

```
@Component({
  selector: 'talks',
  template: `
    <talk *ngFor="let t of app.talks" [talk]="t"\
(selected)="talkSelected($event)"></talk>
  `
})
class TalksCmp {
  constructor(public app: App) {}

  selectedTalks = [];

  talkSelected(e) {
```

```
      this.selectedTalks.push(e.selected);
  }
}

@Component({
  selector: 'talk',
  template: `
    {{talk.title}} {{talk.speaker}}
    {{talk.rating | formatRating}}
    <button (click)="select()">Select</button>
  `
})
class TalkCmp {
  @Input() talk: Talk;
  @Output() selected = new EventEmitter();

  select() {
    this.selected.next({selected: this.id});
  }
}
```

In this example, the talk input of `TalkCmp` is the state, which is derived from the `talks` property of the app object.

Note that we only care about the most recent value of `talk`, that is, skipping an intermediate value of `talk` won't affect anything. Contrast it with the `selected` event sequence, where every single emitted value matters, including the order in which they are emitted.

Time

Another thing that is different in regards to the state and events is their relation to time.

Using time when deriving the state is rarely practical, that is, time is always implicit. Using time when dealing with events is common (for example, debouncing), that is, time is often explicit.

To make dealing with time easier, Angular has support for reified reactive programming.

What is it?

Reified and transparent

Let's look at this example one more time.

```
@Component({
  selector: 'talk',
  template: `
    {{talk.title}} {{talk.speaker}}
    {{talk.rating | formatRating}}
    <button (click)="select()">Select</button>
  `
})
class TalkCmp {
  @Input() talk: Talk;
  @Output() selected = new EventEmitter();

  select() {
    this.selected.next({selected: this.id});
  }
}
```

Or to be more specific, let's look at the `{{talk.title}}` binding. Angular does not provide any object representing it—we only get the current value. We can call this type of reactive programming **transparent** because the developer only interacts with the most recent value, and the act of observation is hidden in the framework.

When propagating state we only care about the latest value, and we don't usually need to worry about time. And that's why Angular uses this type of reactive programming here. It is simpler and a lot more performant. Plus we can use "plain" JavaScript to compose different values changing over time, like this:

```
{{talk.title + ' by ' + talk.speaker}}
```

Now, let's look at the selected event. Angular gives us a `EventEmitter` object to represent it. We can call this type of reactive programming **reified** because we have access to a concrete object representing the act of observation. And having these concrete objects is powerful because we can manipulate them, pass them around, and compose them. In particular, we can use them to explicitly handle time.

This type of reactive programming is more powerful, but it is also more complicated: we have to use special operators to do composition. For instance, the preceding example will have to be rewritten like this:

```
const talk: Subject<{title: string, speaker: string}> = getTalk();
const title: Subject<string> = talk.map(c => c.title);
const speaker: Subject<string> = talk.map(c => c.speaker);
const result: Subject<string> = zip(title, speaker).map(p => `${p[0]} by
${p[1]}`);
```

When handling events we often care about the time aspect, and that's why Angular uses this type of reactive programming for managing events.

Observables

There are many ways to implement event streams or reified reactive programming. Angular embraced RxJS, and the `EventEmitter` class is just an implementation of RxJS/Observable.

RxJS and reactive programming

When saying "reactive programming", many are referring to programing using RxJS. Most of what you do in Angular is reactive even if you don't use RxJS. Reified reactive programming is a better way to refer to programming using observable-based APIs.

What about event callbacks?

Since reified reactive programming is more complicated than transparent reactive programming, Angular supports handling events in a more traditional way by supplying callbacks (for example, the `click` handler in the preceding example). In other words, we can use both transparent and reified programming to handle events. We will see the same being true in other parts of the framework and the ecosystem: we can use transparent reactive programming for simple use cases, and the reified one for advanced ones.

 Unfortunately, at the moment Angular's support for reified reactive programming in the core framework is a bit inconsistent (for example, all the DOM events are handled in the transparent way, but there is a proposal to make it complete `https://github.com/angular/angular/is sues/13248`).

Reactive programming in the Angular ecosystem

We have looked at how the Angular core framework itself supports reactive programming. Now let's look at the Angular ecosystem.

@angular/forms

Angular has always had strong support for building dynamic forms. It's one of the main reasons the framework got so successful.

Now the framework comes with a module that adds support for handling input using reified reactive programming.

```
import {ReactiveFormsModule, FormGroup, FormControl} from '@angular/forms';

@Component({
  selector: 'filters-and-talks',
  template: `
    <form [formGroup]="filtersForm">
      Title <input formControlName="title">
      Speaker <input formControlName="speaker">
    </form>

    <talk *ngFor="let t of talks|async" [talk]="t"></talk>
`
})
class TalksAndFiltersCmp {
  filtersForm = new FormGroup({
    title: new FormControl(''),
    speaker: new FormControl('')
  });

  talks: Observable<Talk[]>;

  constructor(backend: Backend) {
    this.talks = this.filtersForm.valueChanges.
      debounceTime(100).
      switchMap(filters => backend.fetch(filters));
  }
}

@NgModule({
  declarations: [TalksAndFiltersCmp, TalkCmp],
```

```
  imports: [
    ReactiveFormsModule
  ]
})
class AppModule {}
```

Look at how elegant this solution is. We simply define a form with two controls, which we bind to the two input elements in the DOM.

Then we use the `valueChanges` observable to wait for the form to get stable before firing a request. We use the `switchMap` operator to ignore all the requests but the last one, so the filters form and the data will never get out of sync. We then bind the created observable using the async pipe to display the list of talks.

Implementing this without `ReactiveFormsModule` requires a lot of manual state management, correlation IDs, and is not easy to get right. That's why `ReactiveFormsModule` is one of the most useful additions to the framework. It enables us to solve many input-handling problems in an elegant way, with just a few lines of code.

For simple cases, however, we can still grab the current value, which is transparently kept in sync with the UI, like this:

```
@Component({
  selector: 'filters',
  template: `
    <form [formGroup]="filtersForm">
      Title <input formControlName="title">
      Speaker <input formControlName="speaker">
    </form>

    <talk *ngFor="let t of talks|async" [talk]="t"></talk>
  `
})
class TalksAndFiltersCmp {
  filtersForm = new FormGroup({
    title: new FormControl(''),
    speaker: new FormControl('')
  });

  //...

  onSubmit() {
    const currentValue = this.filtersForm.value;
  }
}
```

@angular/router

The Angular router is built around the same ideas. It gives us a simple API to get the current value of params to use in simple use cases, and an observable-based API for more interesting situations.

```
class ItemCmp {
  item: Observable<Item>;

  constructor(route: ActivatedRoute, backend: Backend) {
    this.item = zip(route.paramMap, route.queryParamMap).map(p =>
      backend.fetchItem(p[0].get('id'), p[1].get('loadDebugInfo'))
    );

    route.snapshot.paramMap; // current value;
    route.snapshot.queryParamMap; // current value;
  }
}
```

It also exposes all router events via an observable that can be used as follows:

```
@Component({
  template: `
    <spinner *ngIf="showSpinner|async"></spinner>
  `
})
class AppCmp {
  showSpinner: Observable<boolean>;
  constructor(r: Router) {
    this.showSpinner = r.events.
      // Fitlers only starts and ends.
      filter(e => isStart(e) || isEnd(e)).

      // Returns Observable<boolean>.
      map(e => isStart(e)).

      // Skips duplicates, so two 'true' values are never emitted in a row.
      distinctUntilChanged();
  }
}
```

Summary

An Angular application is a reactive system. And that's why we need to understand reactive programming to be productive with Angular.

Reactive programming works with event streams and the state. And it can be divided into transparent and reified.

Since the very beginning the framework has had excellent support for transparent reactive programming. It was used both to propagate the state and to handle events. It is simple and fast. And the new versions of the framework still support it.

But it can also be limiting at times and make solving certain problems difficult. That's why Angular now comes with support for reified reactive programming, using observables.

The Angular ecosystem embraced these ideas as well. The reactive forms module, the router, and other libraries like NgRx, all provide observable-based APIs.

Index

@

@angular/forms 90
@angular/router 92

A

Ahead-of-time (AOT) 8
Angular application
  bootstrapping 18
Angular Augury
  URL 44
Angular ecosystem
  @angular/forms 90
  @angular/router 92
  reactive programming 90
Angular
  change detection 53
AOT compilation
  about 9
  advantages 9
  trade-offs 10
Apollo
  URL 30

B

bootstrap components 14

C

change detection
  about 49, 52
  in Angular 53
ChangeDetectionStrategy.OnPush 55
compilation 7
components
  about 21
  host element 25
  input property 22
  life cycle 24
  output property 22
  providers, defining 25
  querying 27
  template 23
content children 27, 54

D

dependency injection
  about 37
  aliasing 47
  dependencies, injecting 40
  dependency, marking as optional 45
  overrides 47
  providers, registering 40, 46
  resolution 41
  visibility, controlling 45
directives 28
DOM 74

E

entry components 14
event bindings
  about 32, 49
  two-way bindings 33
events
  about 86
  callbacks 89
  defining 86
  observables 89
  reactive programming, with RxJS 89

F

Falcor
  URL 30
form directives

about 67
form model, accessing 72
FormsModule 70
ReactiveFormsModule 68
form handling 74
form model
about 59
async validations 63
changes, controlling 65
disabling 63
FormArray 61
FormControl 60
FormGroup 60
need for 66
updating 62
validators, composing 64
with RxJS 66

H

high-level overview, forms
app model 58
DOM 59
form directives 59
form model 58
host element
about 25
advantages 26

I

injector tree
about 40
visualizing 44
injector
obtaining 43
integration testing 81
isolated tests 77

J

Just-in-time (JIT) 8

L

lazy loading 19, 42

M

module initialization 18

N

NgModules
declarations 13
exports 13
imports 13
injecting 18

P

property bindings 49, 52
protractor tests 83
providers
about 17
defining, for components 25
registering 39

R

reactive programming
about 85
events 86
in Angular ecosystem 90
reified reactive programming 88
state 86
time, using 87
transparent reactive programming 88
reified reactive programming
about 88
reference 89
RxJS
using, with form model 66

S

shallow testing 79
state 86

T

templates, Angular
* syntax 34
about 32
constants, passing 34
event bindings 32

interpolation 33
properties 32
references, defining 34
templates
analyzing 30
building, on existing technologies and
communities 31
dynamic and static parts, separating 31
implementations, swapping 30
need for 29
reference 29
transforming 30
tests
integration testing 81
isolated tests 77

protractor tests 83
shallow testing 79
transparent reactive programming 88
two modules 57
two phases
about 49
separation 52
separation, for performance 53
separation, for predictability 52
two-way bindings 33

V

validators
composing 64
view children 27, 54

www.ingramcontent.com/pod-product-compliance
Lightning Source LLC
Chambersburg PA
CBHW060200060326
40690CB00018B/4187